The Little Book of Prayer

Michael R. Forry

Edited by
Diana Ceseñas

DEDICATION

For my son Connor, who with his penetrating insight and depth of spirit at 10-years old, forced me to consider carefully what he was being told and what it really means.

CONTENTS

ACKNOWLEDGMENTS

Painfully, insightfully and lovingly edited by Diana Ceseñas, with the care of a mother watching over the spiritual feeding of her son.

1 THE DILEMMA

Success in life often leads us to believe that we are doing all the right things, and the longer we continue along that path, the more we believe only in ourselves. While having confidence and believing in yourself is a good thing, at some point in life, there will be a realization that these normal life pursuits <u>of themselves</u> are hollow. Sadly, this realization is often triggered by some crisis, forcing a life reevaluation. It may be possible for a contemplative or introspective person to arrive at this understanding earlier and possibly without the required crisis, but either way we will come to the conclusion that there has to be more to life than just satisfying our individual desires. This is the 'teachable point'. What you do with it is up to you.

When faced with such a life crisis or challenge, a capable person will consider the choices, the available resources, and work their way through the problems to a successful result, which is admirable (and expected). However, when we charge ahead in life with this narrow focus to the neglect of our spiritual life, we are cultivating the very problem that brought us to the crisis point in the first place.

Is there a better way? Is it all about the destination, crisis management, damage control and moving forward; or is the journey just as important? Could you still get to your destination, but this time everyone could be inside the car instead of hanging on the bumper? What would make a difference?

Prayer

Sounds overly simple, but prayer is the only real answer to the bigger picture of life. Sad, but to most people, it carries about the same weight as luck.

Even to most Christians it is something they throw out as a reflex. Something like saying "Nice to meet you" when it wasn't; "the food is good" when it isn't; "I'll pray for you" when I won't. But it is the right thing to say so you can politely leave the room.

What is Prayer?

Prayer is the sincere desire of your spirit to "come home", to spiritually 'sit in dad's lap'; it is the language of respect, dependence and submission. To not pray is trying to live independently of God, which was the first curse, and continues to be the great curse of mankind. In the beginning, Satan said "Eat this fruit and you shall be as God" (independent of God). Most people continue this failure of living independently of God by either not praying or going through the motions of prayer without engaging the spirit of prayer.

Most have never learned <u>HOW</u> to pray and so they have never SEEN the power of prayer.

Is it really that hard?

Well Jesus gave us a road map, but we just can't manage to unfold it. He laid out the plan in the Lord's Prayer, but it still seems so foreign. Even when explained in detail, it is still hard to grasp.

Maybe it is because we are starting in the wrong place. Instead of reciting a formula, or some "official cook book" way to ask for something, maybe it has to start with something a little deeper, something *within us*.

.

2 RELATIONSHIP

God knows everything about us; and we may have a little knowledge of Him. However few have taken the time to build a relationship with Him. Since we cannot see, hear or touch a relationship it is very hard to understand it; *apart from Jesus and the Holy Spirit we probably never will.*

Why? Because you have something like two different species that **can't** talk to each other; just as humans can't talk to cockroaches.

God made the earth; and then He made man to essentially have someone to share it with and hang-out with (so to speak). But man disobeyed God, which ended that relationship and sent man on his own way of 'independence', separate from God. Man immediately realized this was a death sentence, but there was no way out. However, *someone* had to pay the price to 'bail-out' man from his jail. God wanted so badly to bring his children back home that he allowed his only Son to take the blame. With Jesus taking the punishment, the rest of us could get out of our jail sentence.

But He didn't stop there. For Him, it wasn't enough just to get us out of jail, He wanted His family back. With that bailout, He also created a completely new species, an entirely new "family line". This new family consists of the newly adopted children of Jesus, which cuts off the relationship to the old "cockroach" family line descending from Adam. Those who choose to be adopted by Jesus by accepting and acknowledging Jesus as their savior will become a part of His new family. For now, we are stuck with the body from our old family, but our spirit is now part of the new family. Later, we will get new bodies when we go to be with God and our new family.

With that new spiritual family comes a new way of communicating; through the Holy Spirit; what a wonderful birthday gift! Yes, because we have been adopted by Jesus, the very Spirit of God is now able to communicate with us, from his Spirit to ours…but we have to learn how to listen through a new set of 'ears'. Like babies, this takes time, communication and a consistent relationship to learn His 'language' and voice. In addition, the Holy Spirit is available to guide, teach, and lead us throughout this life.

If you were born into a family, but from the time of birth, never listened or talked to your family members', could you even understand what they were saying? Would you ever know what you were hearing, what guidance was being provided? For that matter, could you really be considered part of that family? We have been provided a way to talk to our new family, and we have a whole new 'language' to learn, but that can only happen by spending time with them, and that happens through prayer.

Absolute Honesty

Here is another challenge, as we learn to 'hear' our new language; we have to learn to spiritually speak with absolute honesty. Shouldn't be so hard, right?

Sounds funny, but being honest can really be hard. You have to admit things about yourself that perhaps you don't want to, face what you are REALLY thinking, feeling, believing, and question if you are even being honest with yourself. The only person that knows that is you, and it should be no surprise that God knows it too, actually better than you do. There is no chance to fool, bluff, lie, or dance around the truth, so you might just as well start learning how to approach God with nothing but an honest heart, because He knows.

3 HOW TO PRAY

Ok, so now that you are in this new relationship, speaking with absolute honesty in a new language (even though it is still baby talk), we now have a foundation for prayer. Prayer requires more of the *heart* than of the *tongue*. Prayer is sincerity and simplicity of faith; which is why Jesus encouraged us to pray like children. God knows, so you don't have to *inform* Him. Prayer is our chance to connect our spirit with God's Holy Spirit, submit our will to His and to remind us that THERE is our Father, our country, and our inheritance. Jesus gave us a model in the Lord's prayer, so when in doubt, follow the directions!

The Lord's Prayer
Someone asked Jesus how to pray. He gave the answer in Matthew 6, verse 5. He starts with a few don'ts and then a few do's.

First the don'ts: don't do it for a show or for appearances (it was big in those days and still is for some). Also, don't recite some memorized thing like a chant or poem; it means absolutely nothing, might as well recite a cookie recipe out loud. It should also not include any crosses, statues, beads or other 'stuff'. God told man not to do that because He cannot be represented by any 'thing'.

Now the Do's: Jesus tells us that this is just between you and God, so go somewhere quiet and private; and when you do, pray this way:

Our Father which art in heaven,
Hallowed be thy name.
Thy kingdom come. Thy will be done on earth, as it is in heaven.
Give us this day our daily bread.
And forgive us our trespasses, as we forgive those who trespass against us.
And lead us not into temptation, but deliver us from evil

Jesus also did not say "pray this" like some poem to be repeated. He said "pray this way". So what exactly does this way mean? Let's break this down into some detail so you can see not just the words, but the meaning, attitudes and reasons behind this simple but powerful prayer map.

BASIC ELEMENTS OF THE LORD'S PRAYER

Attitude and Perspective
Our Father which art in heaven

<u>Respect and Thankfulness</u>. This is a natural reaction when you realize where you are. This is not some sort of vending machine; you are in the presence of the creator of the universe. Not a president or a king, nothing that trivial; no human comparison is possible. You are in front of the Throne of God…this is BIG.

Once you begin to grasp that you are in front of the throne of God, you begin to understand the degree of respect that is due. With the right attitude of respect, you have a good beginning.

Worship – for who He IS
Hallowed be thy name.

What is worship? Worship is really just recognizing the values and attributes of what is in front of you, without regard to any benefits you may receive. Worship is telling God you love Him for *who He is*, not *what He does* for you. On a human level, if someone were to complement you on your generosity, smile, intelligence or wit, it would be just about you and not provide any benefit to the person offering the comment; just the simple recognition of the truth about that person and their nature. Worship is clearly not attempting to butter-up God for something you want; remember that whole honesty thing, well yeah, God can see right through that nonsense. If you can't see through what you are trying to do, then the only one you are fooling is yourself and wasting your time. It's a funny thing that the more you see of His kingdom, the greater prayer has a passion for God's glory and agenda, the more He will have the top priority.

So does God NEED your worship? Does he have some personality issue and a need to be complimented? That is obviously ridiculous and disrespectful. While it is nice to be recognized for who you are, God asks for our worship for <u>our</u> benefit. How is that?

Worship helps *us* to understand the significance of:
- Where we are
- What our attitude should be and

- The kind of requests we should focus on

Worship provides us an opportunity to realize that this is not rattling off a shopping list, but a respectful opportunity *to be before the throne of God.* That realization should cause us to reconsider what we are going to place before Him. So instead asking for that Ferrari, I should be more interested in things like the spiritual health and direction of my family, turning our nation's leaders back to a foundation of faith in God (or changing leadership), and so on.

Realizing you are before the throne of God will shape your thoughts and prayers and worship will take on a natural awe. You will realize that you are in a place where power and authority reside.

Worship is an opportunity to *pause* and *consider* more deeply exactly *who* you are talking to:
- His power in the creation around you
- His amazing brilliance in the complexity and beauty of the things created
- His wonderful attributes of Love, Patience and Kindness
- His sense of *humor* (yes, if you are alert to it He has an amazing sense of humor)

Submission
Thy kingdom come.
Thy will be done on earth as it is in heaven.

A traditional phrase in the prayers of Jesus time was to say "the kingdom of your Messiah come". Jesus didn't say the 'of your Messiah" part because He was fulfilling that request right before their very eyes, *the creation of a new kingdom ruled by*

Jesus. Now that Jesus has created a new kingdom, we get to participate in asking for his kingdom to rule on this earth. Maybe you have seen enough of mans' corrupt and incompetent leadership to realize this is time for a change, and you have been given a chance to make it happen. No matter how young you are, you have a chance to vote in this election, to vote for God's rule on this earth. We don't want things to run according to men's standards and control any more, we want God to be in charge down here, so stand-up and vote for His rule, for His will to be done.

Our desire should be for the kingdom of God and his righteousness to be in charge on this earth, just like it is in heaven. Say it with a heart of perfect love and trust: "Do Your will, because I know it is the best. Change me where I don't understand Your will which I accept with a heart of trust and thankfulness."

Why does God want us to pray that His will be done? He is more than able to do His will without our prayer or cooperation; yet He *allows us the unique privilege of participating* in the accomplishment of His goals through our prayers, and then he lets us see His will be done on earth as it is in heaven. This is like our earthly fathers allowing us to work on a car with them. They could do the task much more easily and quickly without our bumbling efforts getting in the way, but they want to share that experience with us and provide us with a learning opportunity. How much greater the Father wants us to learn and grow with Him.

Thanks, Praise and Requests
Give us this day our daily bread.

God does care about everyday things such as our daily bread (jobs, housing, food, relationships, etc) and we should pray about them. By now, you should have a better idea on how and what to ask for, and as you do, think about this: God made EVERYTHING, rules over everything and he is not broke. All things are under his control and available to him. So Everything and Anything is at his disposal. But God not only HAS everything, he KNOWS everything as well.

Your Father in heaven knows what you need before you ask him so there is no need for long discussions. God uses prayer as a way for you to recognize your need of him and dependence on him. So open your case, pour out your hearts before him, and then leave it with Him. Prayer should be easy, natural, and unaffected; children do not need to make long speeches to their parents when they want anything; they know a simple word will get the message across. Some of the most heartfelt prayers are simply a groan or a sigh. He knows what that means and waits patiently for us to bring those things to Him. If He does not provide what we ask, it is because He knows we are not ready for it, do not really need it or that it would not be good for us; something He can judge infinitely better than we can.

Now that you have the proper attitude and realize exactly where you are standing and whom you are talking to, it would be a good time to be thankful for the things you *have already received* (and perhaps for the things you did not receive because you are not ready). Once you start to realize how thankful you should be, praise may naturally flow out of you.

While you should respectfully say thank you for all the "stuff" you have received, it is even more important to be thankful for the things you cannot see, for example:

- First and foremost, His unbelievable *grace* and *love* for you in providing His own Son to take the punishment for your screw-ups so you can rejoin His family
- His *patience* in waiting for you to "get it"
- His *kindness* in not squashing you like a bug when you are disobedient;
- His willingness to provide for you in abundance
- His wisdom in not providing those very same things to you until you are ready for them
- His wonderful and wise plan for your life
- And all the material things He has provided according to our ability to manage them. As our wise Father, he does not give shotguns to infants and cases of cookies to children. He knows that given the chance, we would just damage ourselves, so He provides as we mature and are able to manage these things without spinning out of control.

So when we bring these things before the Father, with all the appropriate respect and thankfulness for His plan, we have to do so with Faith. Faith is not luck, it is not throwing darts in the dark; it is confidence.

- Confidence that God is able to do whatever he wills.
- Confidence that as a son in the new family, He wants me to live in abundance.
- Confidence in Him, and His ability to provide those things;

- Confidence that He will NOT provide those things if they would become an obstacle to my relationship with Him.

So when you appear before the throne of God and place these requests with Him, realize that the requests stay there and you leave. No doubt you will daydream about these things throughout the day, and that moment is the perfect opportunity to stop, quickly turn your heart to God and thank Him for the perfect plan He is working out for those things, and again leave them there with Him.

Does that mean that you cannot work towards things you want? Such as researching, practicing, exercising or learning anything after you bring it to God, I have to just sit around and wait? That is definitely not the way to go!

So do I pray, then jump up and spring into action? Can't I just pray, pack and go? This should not come as a surprise, but God plays on a board bigger than we can possibly imagine. He is patient to let other things take shape so that several things can come together all at the right time. _Our_ plan may figure that we need money and a place to live. _His_ plan might include not only the resources (such as money, jobs, properties, etc.) to make that happen, but He is also working in other people's lives. _We_ think of things and activities but God has different priorities; He wants to provide opportunities for other people to join to His new family. If we could just pause and be patient to watch Him work, we would be amazed to see His plan unfold in ways that we never would have imagined. And what has he asked us to do? Pray, Believe and be Patient....a really amazingly light load, but sometimes very hard for us, the spoiled and impatient children. When it is His time, he will provide the guidance we need, which is all the more reason for us to be continually listening in prayer so we will see the opportunities that He has laid out before us.

The work is still yours to do, however the decision and direction is not. It is up to you to bring those things to God, leave the decision and direction to Him, and then you can go back to researching your real estate, practice your surfing, pottery, music, business, contracts or whatever. Just realize that what you are doing is just exercise and practice, the actual game and direction will be decided by Him. For example, if your prayer was for a home for your family, if He lines everything up, but you are not even bothering to look for the property, how could you even know that He has made one available? And if you prayed for winning a competition but you have not bothered to exercise and practice, what good will you be when He provides the opportunity to be in that big competition? So it is not a case for 'here is my prayer, now pass me the remote'. God will provide a way and a means when the timing is right, but you need to be ready when the time comes.

When you bring something to God, you have to leave it there and trust him for the decisions and direction. When you come back to the throne, you should thank God for his plan that He is working out for that issue. You should continually thank Him for what he is doing, *whether you see progress or not*, because seeing something does not require faith, and He would rather see you *trust* Him for what you <u>cannot</u> see than celebrate what you <u>can</u> see.

You may ask: Is there anything else I can do? Without a doubt, yes. Throughout the day as thoughts of a particular item or request come to mind, the first thing you should do is make sure you have left that with Him, and then launch immediately into thanks for His plan.

Forgiveness
And forgive us our trespasses,
as we forgive those who trespass against us.

Jesus then reminds us that if we can't forgive everyone else, than we can't expect God to forgive us either. Anyone who recognizes he is truly forgiven will show forgiveness to others. Once our eyes have been opened to see the enormity of our offence against God, the things others have done to us appear extremely small by comparison. If, on the other hand, we have an exaggerated view of the offences of others, it proves that we have minimized our own offenses against God.

Help in Daily Living
And lead us not into temptation, but deliver us from evil

Temptation literally means a test, not necessarily a solicitation to do evil. God has promised to keep us from any testing that is greater than what we can handle. God allows his children to pass through periods of testing for the purpose of their growth and development.

Temptations or tests can begin as a simple disobedient thought. It may not seem like that big of a deal;
- I don't want to listen
- I'll be rich
- I'll get back at them
- I'll be a star and have all that stuff.

Somehow, it will center on 'me'. The Holy Spirit will nudge you to bring that thought to God by asking his forgiveness and help in overcoming that weakness. If left to continue, that thought will turn into a strong imagination, then will grow into our own full-length feature starring us. Eventually that daydream will turn into a far uglier reality as we consent to perform it. Obviously, the best plan is to get rid of the disobedient thought before it grows by bringing that weakness before God as soon as possible. As you submit to God in the middle of those tests, your own strength will grow. God will provide you with even bigger dreams, but this time He will be in charge.

How often should I pray

It is a bit telling of a relationship when the phrasing is "how often do I HAVE to pray?" A better disposition might be 'should I ever stop?' If I were to ask the same question of being around a new girl or boy friend, the question might sound more like 'can I spend the whole day with her' or 'I can't stand to be away from him'. If we see prayer as an obligation or task then we need to work on our relationship. If anything, that might signal that we need to spend even more time in prayer to get to know God in order to realize why we should want to spend every waking moment with Him by our side. No, you are not going to be some sort of monk, but you will have a continual awareness of God's presence, learning how to listen to the guidance of the Holy Spirit throughout the day with frequent moments of thanks to the Father, and the Son. This daily walk would not replace the need for a daily (or multiple daily) period where you slip away to your private prayer session, which would provide a more quiet one-on-one prayer time.

No matter how long you have been a member of God's new family, you are still a baby in His eyes; talking in fractured sentences, taking wobbling steps and frequently falling down. He is a proud Father, always welcoming you with open arms, yearning to hear you, forgive you and provide for your every need when you come home to Him in trusting prayer.